Paint the Prisons Bright

HEROES OF THE FAITH

CORRIE TEN BOOM

Paint the Prisons Bright

JILL BRISCOE

WORD
Kids!

WORD PUBLISHING
Dallas·London·Vancouver·Melbourne

PAINT THE PRISONS BRIGHT

Text copyright © 1991 by Jill Briscoe. Illustrations copyright © 1991 by Jane Wrede.

Library of Congress Cataloging-in-Publication Data

Briscoe, Jill.
    Paint the prisons bright: Corrie Ten Boom / by Jill Briscoe.
        p.   cm. — (Heroes of the faith)
    Summary: Relates events in the life of the Dutch woman who survived imprisonment in Nazi concentration camps to become a Christian missionary.
    ISBN 0–8499–3308–0
    1. Ten Boom, Corrie—Juvenile literature. 2. Christian biography—Netherlands—Juvenile literature. [1. Ten Boom, Corrie. 2. Missionaries.] I. Title II. Series: Heroes of the faith (Dallas, Tex.)
BR1725.T35B74   1991
269'.2'092—dc20
[B]   91–21395
                                        CIP
                                          AC

Printed in the United States of America

1 2 3 4 9 LBM 9 8 7 6 5 4 3 2 1

To our grandchildren,
praying that this story
will help you to know
that Jesus will be
with you when days are
dark and difficult.

Contents

Acknowledgments

With thanks to Kappie Griesell for her help in researching the adventures of Corrie ten Boom, to Jane Wrede for bringing Hark to life with her delightful illustrations, to Sue Ann Jones for her marvelous job of editing, and to Laura Minchew of Word Publishing for her guidance and support of this project. Thanks also to Pamela Rosewell Moore for her help and encouragement—and especially for her prayers in behalf of this book.

1

Soldiers at the Door

Suddenly there was a knock at the door, as loud as thunder.

"It's happening!" Hark the Herald Angel wrote quickly in his notebook. He was invisible, on special assignment from heaven. His job was to gather details that were missing from the record of Corrie ten Boom, a special servant of the King.

Hark had gone back in time to the days of the Second World War. What he was seeing had already happened. So he knew he could not change anything. Nor could he help anyone.

This was hard for Hark because he also knew that terrible things would happen to

Corrie and her family in the days ahead. He knew all that. But sometimes—such as now, with the angry knocks sounding at the door—he became so caught up in the action, he forgot.

"Oh no! I've been so worried this would happen!" he wrote with a shaky angel hand. "A spy has gone to the Nazi enemies. Now they know Corrie is hiding Jews, the people the Nazis hate so much. And now the Nazi soldiers are here!"

A second later, the door burst open with an awful crash. Upstairs, Hark could hear the quiet but frantic scurry of feet as startled guests ran to hide in the secret room.

"Where are the Jews?" a tall, angry soldier shouted as he pushed past Betsie, Corrie's sister. "We know they are here. Where are you hiding them?"

2

2

The Briefing

Hark's adventure had begun when the recording angel, lovingly known as C. D., noticed a few gaps in one of his heavenly records.

"I must make plans to fill in the blanks at once," he said. He went to find Hark, who was just leaving choir practice.

"How would you like an exciting earthly assignment?" he asked the small angel.

"You mean go to earth—all on my own?" Hark gasped, looking quite shocked. "Do you want me to sing there?"

C. D. smiled. He loved to hear Hark the Herald Angel sing! But he answered, "No, I don't need you to go to earth to sing, Hark."

"You don't?" Hark said in surprise. "Then what do you want me to do?"

"Write," replied C. D.

"Write!" Hark exclaimed. "I don't know if I can do *that*."

"All you need to do is travel back and forth through time and collect the data for me. I'll write it up when you bring it back," C. D. explained. "I'll show you how to use the heavenly camera, and I know you'll be really excited to meet Corrie."

"Corrie who?" asked Hark, really interested now.

"Corrie ten Boom," C. D. said softly. "She is one of the King's special servants."

Hark was pleased to know C. D. thought he could do this special assignment. (He would have been proud, too, except no one's proud in heaven.)

"I'll do it," he announced in a very loud voice. It was so loud it startled some little cherubs who were painting flowers on the heavenly pages of C. D.'s huge book.

C. D. turned an earthly globe slowly in the air. He pointed to a small country in Europe between Belgium and Germany called The Netherlands, or Holland. The people who live there are called the Dutch, C. D. explained.

He put his finger on a town. "This is Haarlem, Hark," he said. "This is where you are going." Hark carefully wrote down the name and made sure he knew which part of Corrie's story was missing.

"Set me off in the right direction, please, C. D.," he said. Hark turned around to say goodbye to the cherubs. They gave him some funny-looking shoes called clogs that many Dutch people wore. The cherubs laughingly helped Hark put them on his angel feet. "Now you look ready for Holland!" they said.

"Well, off I go," Hark said stoutly. With one last wave goodbye, he set off toward earth.

The enemy tries his best to stop heroes and heroines of faith who follow Jesus, Hark reflected as he traveled at angel speed through the stars. Little did he know that his heavenly notepad would soon be full of those awful things the enemy liked to do! But it would also be full of King Jesus' love and power on behalf of those who suffer for their faith.

Hark's thoughts were interrupted by his sudden arrival in The Netherlands. Distracted by his thoughts, he hit the ground a little harder than he had intended. But the wooden clogs helped to break his fall. "It's a good thing nobody can see me," he said to himself. "A policeman might have stopped me for speeding!"

He wandered through the land for a bit. He took some photos of the whirling windmills that turned slowly in the wind. He admired the canals that laced the land together and the dikes built to hold back the sea.

Hark used lots of his heavenly film on the incredibly bright fields full of red flowers called tulips. They were every-where! And they smelled so sweet, Hark darted from one blossom to another like a bee. He couldn't decide which one smelled best.

Courtesy of The Netherlands Board of Tourism (KURVERS).

Hark in the tulips.

"Now," he said to himself, "I'd better get on with the job!" He flew to Haarlem to look for Corrie's house.

"Well, here it is," Hark said when he was sure he had the right place. "Yes, it's called the Beje," he noted. C. D. had told him the Dutch pronounced it "Bay-yay."

Holland is a land of tulips and windmills.

Hark dug in the pocket of his angel robe and fished out his heavenly calendar watch that showed the year and date. He was pleased to see he had arrived about the time in Corrie's life that was missing in C. D.'s report. Hark glanced at his notes:

Corrie ten Boom

Born: April 15, 1892.

Address: the Beje; Haarlem, Holland; earth.

Family: *Father:* Casper ten Boom, watchmaker. *Mother:* Cor ten Boom. *Four children* (in order of age): Betsie, Willem, Nollie, Corrie.

Religion: A Christian family, committed to serving Jesus, King of heaven.

Hark's reading was interrupted by a quiet knock on the Beje door. The knock also was heard by a dark-haired woman working at a counter covered with parts from watches and clocks.

"Why, that must be Corrie," Hark decided happily. C. D. had told him that Corrie had become the first woman watchmaker in all of Holland.

Corrie quickly dropped her tools, crossed the room, and peeked out the window of the Beje. Then Hark heard her draw in a sharp breath and whisper a quick prayer.

What could it be? Hark wondered as he glided to the window to hover invisibly over Corrie's shoulder. "Oh!" he cried when he saw who stood outside the door (although no humans could hear his angel voice, of course).

Waiting on the doorstep were two young soldiers. They were wearing the uniform of the Nazis, the dreaded German army led by the tyrant Adolf Hitler. The Nazis had taken over most of Europe, including Holland, and they hated anyone who resisted them. But they had a special hatred for the Jews. Hark trembled as he remembered reading in his history book about the awful search-and-destroy mission Hitler had ordered against the Jews. He wanted to kill all of them!

"What could the soldiers want here?" Hark asked himself nervously. He hurried to find his pencil and turn his heavenly notepad to a clean page.

The great adventure was about to begin.

3

A Blessing in Disguise

Seeing the soldiers' uniforms, Hark realized he had arrived in the middle of the Second World War. During those years the Beje was a place where Jews could hide in their desperate attempt to get away from the Nazis. Many Dutch people—including Corrie and her family—were bravely helping the Jews escape from Holland. These people knew Hitler was wrong to treat the Jews so badly.

Hark had arrived at a time when Corrie and Betsie were lovely, middle-aged ladies. They still lived at the Beje with Father ten Boom, who was in his eighties. Mother ten Boom had long since died, leaving her

The Ten Boom children: Betsie (left), Willem, Nollie, and Corrie.

home on earth for her home in heaven. Willem and Nollie were married with families of their own.

Learning her father's trade and becoming Holland's first woman watchmaker was a real honor and showed how clever Corrie was. But her father reminded her that God is the One who gives us our brains to use and our skills to serve others. When tiny watch parts needed repairing, Corrie would pray, "Lord Jesus, will You lay Your hand on my hand?"[1] Together, Jesus and Corrie would make the watch like new again!

Now, as Corrie stepped to the door to face the soldiers, Hark began to get all hot and prickly. He was nervous because he knew the dangerous thing Corrie and her family were doing to save as many Jews as they could. Their work had helped many Jews escape up to this point. But Hark knew there were spies among the Dutch people. One of them might soon find out what the Ten Booms were doing and report them to the Nazis. Maybe that had already happened, Hark thought as Corrie opened the door.

But the two soldiers waiting there were not angry, loud, and rude like the other Nazi soldiers who filled Haarlem these days. Instead, they seemed young and un-sure of themselves. In fact, they looked downright scared, Hark decided.

"Help us, Corrie," one of them begged. "We don't want to fight in Hitler's army anymore. But if we don't, we will be killed just like the Jews are being killed."

"Someone said you would help us get a disguise and papers so we can escape," the other young man whispered urgently.

Corrie quickly pulled them inside.

"Of course," was all she said.

That night Corrie was in Betsie's sewing room busily altering the soldiers' uniforms. Hark noticed they had crooked crosses on the collars that looked like this: ✠ He knew from his heavenly history lessons that the figure was a swastika, the symbol of Hitler's Nazis.

Betsie, coming into the little sewing room, exclaimed, "Why, Corrie, more uniforms? Now we have five. That's wonderful!" She clapped her hands in joy.

Corrie smiled, too. "We can use the uniforms to disguise some of our own secret underground workers, Betsie," she said.

Underground workers didn't actually work underground, Hark learned from Corrie's excited talk with Betsie. He noted carefully in his little book that these people were very brave Dutch folk who were in a secret army. They risked their own lives helping people escape.

Corrie was looking very serious now. "Betsie, we've just heard of an orphanage in Amsterdam that is trying to save 100 Jewish babies from the Nazis. They hope to get all these little ones into Dutch families all over Holland. But the Nazis have found out about the plan, so we must hurry. I thought we could use these uniforms for our workers. They could pretend to be Nazis, go to the orphanage, and rescue the babies!"

"Oh, Corrie, what a splendid idea!" Betsie exclaimed. "Why, they wouldn't be stopped if they were in Nazi uniforms. They could actually pretend to 'arrest' the children. Then they would take the little ones to the safe homes waiting for them."

"When the real Nazis arrive all the babies will have disappeared," added Corrie, her eyes twinkling.

Hark's eyes were twinkling, too—even more than usual. He laughed a wonderful angel laugh. "What a super plan! And what brave people these were," he said aloud (although no one could hear him, of course).

Then his thoughts became solemn. "Why, if the Nazis ever caught the Ten Booms, they would be in terrible trouble.

They might even be sent to one of the awful prison camps. The Nazis filled those evil places with people who dared to speak out against them," Hark said to himself, suddenly nervous. "They say people are killed there."

Betsie went to cook dinner, and Corrie finished altering the Nazi uniforms for the underground workers to wear. Late that evening five young Dutch men slipped into the Beje.

"Thank you, Corrie," one of them said, putting on the Nazi jacket. "Do I look the part?"

"You do," said Corrie. "And may God keep you safe and help you rescue His children."

The next day the five young Dutch men put their daring plan into action. Hark traveled swiftly through time and was ahead of them to record the exciting rescue. The plan worked perfectly. Every single baby was saved!

"If only all the rescue attempts could turn out this way in the days ahead," Hark said to himself. But he knew that was not to be.

4

The Ten Booms' Secret

More and more scared people began to knock at the door of the Beje. All were trying to escape the Nazis. All were welcomed by the Ten Booms. Corrie became very daring and eventually had eighty people working for her in the underground rescue effort.

The Gestapo, the Nazis' dreaded secret police, forced Jews to carry special identity cards marked with a "J." Even worse, they had to wear a bright yellow patch on their clothes. The patch showed a large six-pointed star—the Star of David, a Jewish symbol.

One day Corrie called her father and Betsie together. "We need to make a secret place inside our house. The Jews could hide there if the Gestapo police find out what we're doing and come looking," she said.

"I know a Dutch architect in the underground. He can help us make a secret room," Betsie said excitedly.

"We could smuggle in bricks inside grandfather clocks, pretending the clocks need repair," she added. "Then no one would know we were building anything."

And so, with help from the secret workers, a little room was built by adding a new wall in Corrie's bedroom. Wallpaper was found that exactly matched the paper on the old walls. It was carefully stained and smudged. Then it looked old, just like the paper that was already on the other walls! The baseboards were carefully replaced by a friend who cleverly made them look old, too.

The entrance to the secret room was a small opening on the bottom of the closet's

The Beje. The secret room was in Corrie's bedroom, top left. The watch shop is at the lower right.

back wall. A shelf hung above the sliding panel that served as a tiny door.

"No one will find it!" exclaimed Betsie excitedly. "We'll put water and food inside, and a bucket in the corner for a toilet," she added, ever practical.

The Jews who were secretly staying at the Beje hoped they would never have to use the hiding place. But Corrie and Betsie had everyone practice getting inside it very quickly just in case the Nazis raided the house. Downstairs, Betsie would sound the alarm. Then Corrie would time the guests as they rushed up the stairs to the secret room. Their best practice time was seventy seconds.[2] Corrie hoped it was fast enough.

Next, the sisters needed a way to let Jews know it was safe to come to the Beje.

"It would be awful if a Jewish family knocked on our door while a policeman was here getting his watch repaired," said Corrie.

The tiny opening to the secret room was under a shelf in Corrie's closet.

"Let's use this as a secret signal," suggested Betsie. She pointed to a red-rimmed triangle sign for Alpina watches. "When we stand this in the windows, the Jews will know it's safe to come to the door."

Night after night people came to the Beje. Each person received a loving, warm welcome, food, a bed, fake identity papers, and a disguise for escape. Later the Jews were smuggled out by good Dutch people.

This sign in the Beje window told Jews it was safe to come inside.

This is so risky! Hark worried. *Why, just one person could betray this wonderful Christian family to the Nazis!*

Then came the day when the thundering knock at the Beje door told Hark his fears had come true.

Realizing this was one of the gaps in the record he had come to collect, Hark ran upstairs to see what was happening there. Four Jews and two underground workers were staying at the Beje that day. Nollie was upstairs visiting Father Casper. Willem was upstairs, too, leading a prayer meeting. Corrie was ill. She was sleeping in her bed. Suddenly rough shouts and angry voices filled the Beje as the front door crashed open.

"Quick," shouted a Gestapo officer to his men. "Search the house and catch the Jews that they are hiding here."

Betsie had gone downstairs to answer the door. But the angry men ran by her without stopping. She quickly pressed the button that rang the secret alarm bell upstairs. It told the Beje's guests they were in trouble.

Hark watched, his angel eyes as big as saucers. The four Jews and two Dutch workers ran into Corrie's room and disappeared through the opening under the bottom shelf of her closet. Just as the last foot was tucked inside the hiding place, she slid the shelf into position and slammed shut the closet door. Then she jumped back into bed!

Almost immediately a Gestapo officer came rudely into her room and demanded, "Where are the Jews you are hiding?"

"I don't know what you mean," Corrie gasped, silently praying, *Lord, guard my mouth!* Hark, being an angel, could hear the prayers people prayed even when they weren't prayed out loud. So he wondered greatly why Corrie had prayed such a prayer. He didn't have to wait long to find out, though. The man began to beat Corrie, demanding that she tell him where the Jews were hiding.

Hark wanted to stop the cruelty. But he knew he was seeing something that had already happened in the past, so he could do nothing about it.

Despite the cruel blows, Corrie told the officer nothing. God *had* guarded her mouth, Hark realized.

"Get downstairs," the soldier told Corrie harshly. Corrie pulled on some clothes over her pajamas. Feeling very weak because she was sick—and because of the beating—she stumbled down the stairs. When she arrived, Betsie and Father were seated with the Gestapo police standing over them. Soon Nollie and Willem were brought in, too.

"She's in charge of the whole thing," one policeman said, pointing to Corrie. The man who had beaten Corrie pushed her down into a chair. Her head throbbed from the blows. Betsie looked helplessly at Corrie, her eyes trying to tell her something. Corrie followed her gaze to the window and saw that the secret sign was up, telling Jews it was "safe" to come to the door! The Gestapo officer saw them looking at the window and smiled a cruel smile.

"Yes, your sign is up," he said smoothly. "Your precious sister knocked it down when she saw us. So I knew it had to be important to those Jews you are trying to help. I thought we might catch some more of them if we left it up while we are here." No sooner had he spoken than a knock came at the door.

"Oh no, no!" Corrie said under her breath. The Nazis opened the door and a family of frightened Jews walked right into the arms of the enemy!

That awful day Hark counted almost thirty people who came to the Beje seeking safety. Instead of being saved, the poor souls were captured and taken away to the dreaded prisons. Hark watched helplessly as Father, Corrie, Betsie, Nollie, and Willem were also told to put on their coats. Then they, too, were marched out of the Beje. The Nazis herded them into an army truck for the cruel ride to a dark and terrible place.

Some soldiers stayed behind to guard the Beje—and perhaps capture more Jews. Watching them, Hark suddenly thought of the people in the secret room. *How would they survive?* he worried. *How would they escape?*

5

The Rescue

Running upstairs, Hark walked through the walls (angels can do that very easily) and squeezed into the secret closet. Six terrified people cowered in the small, stuffy space. There was only enough room for four of them to sit at a time.[3] They took turns sitting and standing. No one could sleep.

"The raid happened at the worst possible time," one of them whispered to the others.

"Why?" asked a scared Jewish girl.

"Because someone made a mistake and took the food and water out of here earlier today," he replied in despair.

"Shhh," said one of the Dutch people. "They might hear us!"

"But who will tell us what's going on in the house? And how long will we have to stay here until it's all clear downstairs?" asked an older man in a tiny whisper. Hark felt the fear of the people who were crushed together inside the tiny space.

The torture continued through the next day and the next night, and half a day more. Hark stayed right there with the hungry, thirsty people as they cried and prayed and held on to each other. Minute by minute, they listened for Corrie's voice telling them it was safe to come out. But Hark knew that could not happen. Corrie couldn't tell them to come out because she wasn't there. She had been arrested.

As the long hours dragged by, Hark carefully wrote down every prayer prayed to the King of heaven in that dark place of despair. And he counted each tear. He knew the Bible says that every tear is counted for the record in heaven. So he was careful to get out his heavenly calculator and add up the total number of teardrops. He wanted to get his numbers right!

"One day all tears will be wiped away by the King, Himself," he said gently. Even though they could not hear him, the huddled group seemed to relax a moment as Hark spoke the age-old words of comfort. "In heaven there will be no more tears. Tears belong to time and earth, not to heaven and eternity."

But this *was* earth, not heaven. And downstairs the people who had helped the Nazis were guarding the house. That left the six people trapped in the secret room. Hark counted many more tears before their ordeal was over!

When the Dutch underground heard what had happened, its workers responded quickly.

"We must rescue the trapped people," said the leader. "Two of our men are really Dutch policemen working at police headquarters. We'll send them to the Beje. They can pretend they've come to check it out," he said. "Then they can go upstairs, give the secret password at the closet door, and bring the people out."

Waiting with those people in the tiny secret room, Hark wiped his brow. Again, he had become so wrapped up in the crisis at hand he had forgotten that he knew what was ahead. His angel heart was pounding, and his fingers trembled as he guided the heavenly pencil across the page. He wanted to take good notes so he could fill the gaps in the record. But he was so worried he could hardly think straight.

Would the rescuers get to the people in the hiding place before they died of thirst and hunger? And if they did, could they safely slip them away from the well-guarded Beje? Hark worried.

And where, oh where, were the Ten Booms?

6

Prison

Hark flew all over Haarlem, but he could not find Corrie and her family. At last he found them standing before a Nazi officer in the prison at Scheveningen, a town near The Hague. They were being questioned by the German officers.

One officer was rough and rude to the others, but not to Father Casper. He wanted to let the old man go. Hark's heart beat faster. *Maybe Father Casper is going to escape,* Hark thought. *If only he says the right thing!*

But the other officers insisted that Father Casper be put into a prison cell. There, the old man told the other prisoners, "If I am released tomorrow, I shall go on the day after tomorrow giving aid to the Jews."[4]

Father's words were quickly repeated to the guards.

"Oh dear! That does it," Hark said. He was right. The officer was furious and refused to let the old man go.

The other members of the Ten Boom family were taken away one by one to dark, filthy cells. There they waited for worse things still to come.

"How cruel these human beings are to one another," Hark wrote sadly. He huddled against the wall of Corrie's cell listening to her deep, troubled thoughts. (Angels can hear human thoughts just as if they are spoken out loud.) He heard crying coming from the other cells. And he heard Corrie cry out to the King of heaven, the One who had suffered in prison, Himself. Jesus knew just what it was like. Hark watched Jesus, who promises never to leave His children when they are in trouble, touch Corrie's heart and answer her prayers. He gave her His peace that passes all understanding. Peace was something that only the King of heaven could give in that sad, terrible place.

Hark settled down in the cell with Corrie. He didn't know how long Corrie would be there. He hoped she would soon be set free. Hark kept busy writing down the many things Corrie was thinking and praying about.

"This is such a dark and dirty little cell, God," she said. "But I'm not afraid. I remember when I was a child and was afraid of the dark. I slept with Nollie and she let me hold the hem of her nightgown as I fell asleep. That gave me such courage! Now I can reach up and touch the hem of Your robe. And You will keep me close to You."[5]

Hark thought that was one of the most beautiful prayers he had ever heard. He watched happily as Corrie fell asleep in Jesus' arms.

The days passed slowly, so very slowly, wrote Hark. The darkest day came when Corrie learned her father had died. He had become ill and was taken to a prison hospital. He had died while waiting alone in the hospital hallway for someone to help him.

But there was happiness, too, when Corrie learned that Nollie and Willem had been released. Then a package came from Nollie. The package, itself, gave Corrie comfort. But it was the secret message written under the postage stamp that filled her heart with joy. As she peeled back the stamp with her ragged thumbnail, the tiny script appeared: "All the watches in your closet are safe."[6]

Corrie's face, which had been sad so long, broke into the biggest, happiest grin as her shining eyes read the words. She knew the secret message had nothing to do with watches. It was about the six people who had hidden in her closet on the day she was arrested.

"They're safe! Oh, thank You, Jesus! They were rescued. Now they're safe," she whispered earnestly.

Reassured that Corrie's spirits were lifted, Hark took a moment to look at his notes. He saw that C. D. had already collected details about the rest of Corrie's days in the first two prisons she and Betsie were taken to. It was news about their final prison that C. D. had asked him to add. Undoing his camera, Hark took one last picture of Corrie. She was smiling as she lay on the dirty bed in her tiny cell.

Then Hark packed away his camera and pencil. Slowly he prepared to move on through time to Corrie and Betsie's last prison. He was not anxious to go because the last prison—a prison camp—was the worst place of all.

Ravensbruck.

7

Answered Prayer

Hark dreaded going to Ravensbruck, a terrible Nazi prison camp in Germany. He knew Satan had taken special pleasure in creating ways to hurt and torture people there. He also knew that thousands and thousands of Jews and others had been put to death in that evil camp.

Now Hark would have to live through it all again, just as it had happened in the history of the world. His angel heart beat painfully at even the thought of it.

"How evil is evil—but how good is God," he said aloud to help himself as he neared that awful place.

Hark had heard about the conditions in the prison camps, especially in the big sleeping rooms, called barracks. Hundreds of women sometimes were crammed into dirty, lice-infested beds in the cold, stark barracks. Beds made to hold two people might hold eight! The prisoners had to get up at 4:30 every morning. Then they had to stand outside without warm clothes, waiting for hours in the bitter cold for roll call. It was so cold some prisoners would collapse and die right there on the hard, frozen ground!

Even knowing what to expect, Hark found it very hard to write down all the terrible things he saw at Ravensbruck. He took a few pictures, knowing that without proof no one would believe how bad it really was.

He watched as Corrie and Betsie waited with the other women being checked into the prison camp. Corrie held a little bottle of vitamin oil and the precious Bible God had helped her smuggle past all the other searches and checkpoints so far.

God's Book had helped her so much; she was frightened the guards would find it. She wondered how she would get it past them when the prisoners had to strip naked for the showers. And after that, they would put on thin prison dresses.

As they stood in line for the showers, Corrie asked a guard if they could use the toilet. Instead, the guard sent the two women into the huge shower room, now empty. Corrie and Betsie stood there, alone.

Looking around frantically, Corrie saw a pile of old furniture against a far wall.

"Quick, Betsie! This way!" she whispered.

"Oh, Corrie," Betsie gasped. "It's filthy! And look at all the bugs!"

"Never mind," replied Corrie. "This is the answer to our prayers! Take off your woolen underwear, Betsie," she said to her sister. "You're going to need it later to stay warm." She quickly rolled the little bottle of vitamin oil and the beloved Bible in the underwear. Then she hid the soft package under the furniture.

"We'll be back in here for our showers," Corrie whispered to Betsie. "We can hide these things here while we have to be undressed."

But their worries weren't over. After their shower they had to think of how to get their treasures out again, past yet another search.

"I'll use the Bible and bottle for shoulder pads," Corrie whispered to Betsie. She shoved the items inside the neck of her loose-fitting prison dress. The underwear went inside the dress, too, settling at Corrie's waist. Corrie wondered if she would be caught. The secret parcels seemed to stick out in huge lumps under her dress. She was sure the guards would notice them.

"Oh, Lord, it's so important that Betsie and I keep the woolen underwear, the bottle, and the Bible. Help me!" Corrie whispered to the King of heaven. "Send Your angels to surround me!"

"He heard her, of course," Hark noted in his record. He watched with delight as some of his fellow angels suddenly appeared beside Corrie. They formed an invisible wall around the worried woman.

"But angels are transparent! The guards will look right through you and see Corrie!" Hark cried to the other angels. (No one else could hear him, of course.)

The angels raised their wings to form a shield around Corrie. "We're a special protection squad," one of them replied with a smile. "We may seem transparent to you. But the guards can't see through us at all!"

As the women passed by the guards, the men carefully searched each prisoner. Corrie and Betsie inched nearer the checkpoint.

Then Hark watched happily as Corrie walked right past the guards. She did it again at a second checkpoint, too!

"They can't see Corrie at all!" Hark gasped. "They're stopping everyone else. But she just walked right by them!"

So Corrie and her treasures were saved.[7]

Hark was delighted! He wrote quickly, happy that God's Book, the woolen underwear, and the precious bottle of vitamin oil had been carried safely through the enemy lines.

When Betsie and Corrie got to the awful barracks, they found they would have to share one tiny bed with three other women! The others grumbled. But they let Betsie and Corrie squeeze on to the hard, narrow bed. Soon the poor, trapped, tired women were all asleep.

Watching them, Hark wished he could tell Betsie and Corrie about the good things that would come from these sad prison days. He wished he could tell them that from their tears would come joy.

8

Thank God for Fleas!

Hark turned to a new piece of paper in his heavenly notepad. It was a beautiful notepad, decorated by angels and smelling of heaven. Now Hark was very glad about the smell of heaven because the awful smells around him were making him quite ill. He felt so sorry for the poor women crammed into the barracks where toilets overflowed and where mice, rats, and cockroaches roamed freely. *How do they stand all the creepy crawlers around them?* he wondered. *Why, they even have bugs in their clothes!*

Suddenly he realized Corrie and Betsie were talking about yet another problem.

Some of the women were fighting and arguing with each other.

This would cause trouble for everyone in the barracks if the guards heard the noise. All the women would be punished harshly for what only a few were doing.

Hark saw that no one knew what to do. No one, that is, except Betsie. Some tried whispering, "Sh-h-h-h!" Others tried to calm the arguing women. And in the middle of it all, Betsie was calmly praying. Her head bowed and her eyes closed, she spoke directly to the heavenly Father.

Hark could hear her ask Him to bring peace and love into the crowded room.

"And He did," Hark noted.

As Betsie prayed, the women who had been arguing with each other turned and stretched their necks to see her. Betsie's face had a bright, happy glow as she talked to Jesus. Slowly the women stopped bickering. Suddenly it didn't matter who got the best places on the beds or whether the windows were open or closed.[8]

As they quieted down, Hark marveled at Betsie. She was suffering terribly, just like all the others. But she always tried to find ways to talk to the other women about Christ, her Savior. Instead of dwelling on her own problems, she tried to comfort others and be a peacemaker. Corrie was so thankful she and Betsie were together in their suffering.

One of the things the sisters hated was always being dirty. Sometimes they would be given a shower, but this was something they dreaded. They knew that in the showers, sometimes water came out of the faucets—and sometimes gas came out! This was the way Nazis killed hundreds of people every day in the shower room. They locked the prisoners in the shower room. Then the poison gas came out of the faucets, and the poor prisoners who breathed it died![9]

Corrie and Betsie never knew when they were sent to the showers whether they were going there to be washed—or killed! But as they walked that way one day, Hark noted that Corrie and Betsie were not afraid. He overheard Corrie's silent words: *Why, Lord, I feel Your hand in mine!*

"Betsie," said Corrie one day, "whatever would we do without the comforting words from the Bible we read every day?" She turned to the page for the day and read, "'Encourage the people who are afraid. Help those who are weak. Be patient with every person. Be sure that no one pays back wrong for wrong. But always try to do what is good for each other and for all people.'"

"Yes, that's it!" said Betsie. "Keep reading."

Corrie continued. "It says, 'Always be happy. Never stop praying. Give thanks whatever happens. That is what God wants for you in Christ Jesus.'"[10]

Corrie looked at Betsie in amazement. "What could we possibly give thanks for in this awful place, Betsie?"

"Why, Corrie," Betsie answered with a twinkle in her eye, "let's thank Him for the lice and the fleas!"

Corrie couldn't believe what she was hearing. "*For the fleas?* How could anyone possibly give thanks for fleas?" she demanded.

"They keep the guards away, Corrie," Betsie said. "Don't you see? They won't come around, bothering us at night, because they don't want to get fleas and lice. So that's when we can read the Bible and have our prayer meetings! Haven't you ever wondered why the guards don't patrol around here late at night?"

Corrie looked at her sister in total surprise. She *had* wondered why the guards had never caught them reading the Bible to the women who crowded around their bunks each night. Now she realized Betsie was right.

"Even in this awful place, we can thank God for using fleas to keep the guards away," Betsie said thoughtfully.

The sisters smiled at each other. Then they held hands and prayed for strength to go on being thankful—even for fleas![11]

"Yes," wrote Hark, watching the pair. "God's strength is what's needed most to survive this awful place called Ravensbruck."

9

The Oil Keeps Coming

In this harsh setting, Hark was amazed at Betsie's loving ways. Her whole body showed the terrible strain of the hard work they had to do at Ravensbruck. She grew weaker and weaker every day. But Betsie's strong love and kindness endured.

At roll call Corrie would try to make room for herself and Betsie in the middle of the rows of women. The icy wind was so strong and cold it almost blew the life out of the poor women who got stuck standing at the end of the rows.

One day Betsie said to Corrie, "We should think of others before ourselves, Corrie. We shouldn't try to take the better places for roll call. Someone has to stand on the end!"

Corrie was amazed. "Only Jesus Christ can make you act like this, Betsie," Corrie said.

Day after day things grew worse and worse. The barracks where Corrie and Betsie slept was supposed to hold four hundred women. Instead, fourteen hundred women had to live there! Bunks were stacked to the ceiling, and women had to share the beds. Sometimes they only had a few inches of space on the thin, straw mattress! And for all these women, there were only eight toilets.[12]

In this crowded place, Corrie and Betsie found room for love and kindess. Each night they gathered the women around the precious Bible. They read its words of life and hope.

"Can anything separate us from the love Christ has for us? Can troubles or problems or suffering? . . . But in all these things we have full victory through God who showed his love for us," Betsie read from the Book of Romans.[13]

Then it was Corrie's turn. She chose Jesus' words from the Book of Matthew. "'You can be sure that I will be with you always. I will continue with you until the end of the world.'"[14]

It seemed to be written just for Ravensbruck, Hark thought.

Other women, so weak and ill they were about to die, found help and hope in Betsie and Corrie's Bible reading. They knew Jesus would take them safely home to heaven.

"Death will be the gateway into a new life for you," Corrie told them. "It will be like waking up from a nightmare into a happy place. There will be no more hunger, no beatings, no pain. Heaven is a place where all tears will be wiped away. All bad memories will be erased forever!"

"It will be a place," Betsie added, "where only love, not hate, is known." She told her friends what Father Casper had always told his children.

"He would tell us, 'When Jesus takes your hand, He keeps you tight. When Jesus keeps you tight, He leads you through life. When Jesus leads you through life, He brings you safely home.'"[15]

The dying women clung to these promises. They were happy to know their pain would soon be over.

Every day each poor prisoner was given one piece of black bread to eat. Often that was all they had to eat all day.

"Just imagine trying to live on only a piece of black bread each day," wrote Hark. "No cereal or ice cream. No peanut-butter-and-jelly sandwiches. No angel food cake!"

Betsie was sick. She had never been very strong. Now Corrie was terribly worried about her. But remember God had helped them to smuggle the little bottle of vitamin oil into prison for just this reason!

"It will give strength to these starving women," said Betsie.

"But this will help *you,* Betsie," Corrie said. "I don't want anyone else to have it but you!"

Each morning Corrie would lovingly pour a precious drop of the vitamin oil onto the bread for Betsie.

"How long do you think it will last?" Corrie asked Betsie anxiously.

"I don't know," Betsie replied, coughing badly. "But Corrie, those poor women at the ends of the barracks have awful colds like I do. I gave them some of the vitamin oil today."

"Betsie, we won't have any left for you," Corrie objected.

"But there are so very, very many sick women, Corrie," replied Betsie. "How can I stop giving it to them and keep it all for myself?"

"But the bottle is so small," cried Corrie.

"But God is so big," Betsie answered softly, smiling at her sister.

"Corrie, there was a woman in the Bible who had a little pot of oil. God told her to use it for the prophet Elijah and it didn't run out. Do you remember the story?"[16]

"Yes, of course," replied Corrie. "But wonderful things happened all through the

51

Bible. I don't know if such things happen today for people like you and me," she added wistfully.

"Well, let's see," said Betsie. "Let's pray about it. We should go on sharing our precious vitamin oil with everyone who is really sick. We will trust God to keep the oil coming from the little bottle."

Day after day the women gathered around Corrie and Betsie and watched the precious drops of vitamins drop onto the black bread. Even though the bottle should have been empty, it wasn't. Corrie couldn't believe it—the lifesaving oil just kept coming!

One day Mien, a friend who was also a prisoner at the camp, got assigned to work in the prison hospital. There she managed to smuggle out some vitamins from the hospital kitchen! She brought them to the sisters. Corrie and Betsie couldn't believe such luck.

"Let's finish the drops from our vitamin bottle first," Corrie suggested. That night Hark watched in wonder as Corrie brought out the little bottle of oil. She planned to pour a drop on Betsie's piece of black bread. But the bottle was empty.

"When Mien brought the new vitamins, God was providing for His children another way," wrote Hark. "There was now no need for the little bottle to keep pouring out its oil!"

"How great is our God," Corrie said to Betsie. "Even in this horrible dark place He is looking after us."[17]

10

Betsie's Release

Betsie began to talk about the day of their release. Hark watched his heavenly pencil sharpen itself. Then he reached for his camera and took a few more pictures. *Maybe they won't be here too much longer,* he thought.

He was sad to see how skinny and sick Betsie had become. *The Devil must be glad to see the poor starving people,* thought Hark. *He even likes to see how mean the guards are to the prisoners.*

Hark wondered if Betsie would be able to recover when she was released. (She seemed quite sure she was going to be free by Christmas.)

Early one morning Hark began to listen to the sisters talking. "Corrie, I've been thinking," Betsie said. "I've had a wonderful idea. It's about what we'll do when we get out of here."

"*If* we get out of here," Corrie responded flatly.

"Oh, we will—we will! And Corrie," Betsie continued, "when we're done, we'll have a place for people who have been hurt in the war. It will be a place where they can get better and learn that love overcomes everything."

Hark wrote busily all that day. He also wrote about the difference Betsie and Corrie were making in the grim barracks. The two sisters brought faith and love to the crowded place that looked more like a huge, dirty ant colony than a home for people. In the middle of the room was a big square table where prisoners knitted army socks all day long. Hark admired the way these women learned to pray. Betsie, too sick to work outside in the bitter cold anymore, taught them by her own example.

She led the women in praying even for the guards who were so cruel to them.

"Jesus said we must pray for our enemies and for those who hate us," she reminded them.

"Why, this terrible place has become the pathway to heaven," wrote Hark. He had seen how the women's hearts were opened by their prayers for their enemies. "They are prisoners," he wrote, "but their prayers fly free to the very throne of God!"

Women who were very sick stayed in their beds in the barracks. There was no one to look after them—no one, that is, except Betsie and Corrie and other women whose lives were being changed by God's power. The sisters would pray and share Jesus' love with these poor women.

"Corrie," said Betsie in tears one day. "I've just seen the guards beating a poor woman who was feeble-minded."

"Feeble-minded people are different from most," Hark wrote. He knew they had been born with something wrong in their minds. The Nazis disliked people who were weak or sick or had other health problems. They had decided these people didn't deserve to live. So they brought them to the camps and treated them even worse than the other prisoners. Then they left them to die.

Hark, too, had seen the guards beating the confused young woman. His cheeks were wet with tears, like Betsie's. He felt sorry for these people who couldn't help being the way they were.

Corrie replied, "Why, every single person, however quick or however slow, however normal or however odd, is very special to God! He loves them and has died for them. And one day He will make them perfectly whole in heaven!"

Hark was glad to see how Corrie and Betsie tried to give these people special love and attention, especially when they were mistreated.

"Betsie," Corrie was saying, "when we get out of Ravensbruck, why don't we open the Beje for these people? They can come and live with us!"

"We will, Corrie, we will," Betsie agreed happily. "People like this need to be helped to see that the love of God can overcome hatred."

It took a moment for Corrie to realize that she was thinking about the feeble-minded, while Betsie was talking about the guards who were mistreating them! Betsie knew the guards were sick of mind, as well, and needed healing. But Corrie found it hard to love the guards! They were so cruel to the poor prisoners.

"Corrie, we'll have a beautiful big house in the country for war victims to come to, as well as the Beje," Betsie told her sister one day. Betsie was too sick now to even sit at the big square table and knit socks anymore. But she patiently endured all the pain of her illness. With great joy she described the lovely gardens in the house she saw in her dream. She was so sure God would give such a place to them.

"Ex-prisoners from the camps will be helped so much by being able to walk among God's lovely flowers," she said. "The house will have a winding staircase and statues and tall, tall windows and special wood floors!" she went on.

Corrie looked at her in amazement. Was Betsie so sick she was "seeing things" that weren't there?

"And Corrie," Betsie said, so ill now her voice was barely a whisper, "we'll take one of these dreadful prison camps, too. We'll paint it the bright colors of sunshine and put flowers in every window!"

Now Corrie was sure Betsie's sickness had affected her mind! Use one of these awful places of death and despair? Turn it into a center for hurting people whose lives had been wrecked by war? Impossible!

As though reading her thoughts, Betsie smiled weakly and said, "Nothing is impossible with God, Corrie."[18]

One day when Corrie returned from roll call, Betsie had been taken to the prison hospital by the guards. Fearing the worst,

Corrie ran to the hospital window, scratched away the frost, and peered inside the grim ward. She couldn't see her sister.

Mien, who worked there, called out to her, "Corrie, come this way. I'll take you to see Betsie."

"I'm afraid, Mien," cried Corrie. "I know she's dead."

"Yes, she is," replied Mien very quietly. "But come with me, Corrie. You *must* see her."

Reluctantly, Corrie let Mien take her to see her sister's body. She didn't want to go— not one little bit. But she let Mien lead her to Betsie's small, still form. What she saw took her breath away. Hark, also following along, was amazed, too. He had last seen Betsie in the barracks, a skinny, pale, sick woman. Her cheeks had been sunken. Her hair had been tangled with dirt and lice. Her eyes had been sunken with suffering. Now her body lay peacefully, suffering no more. But it was Betsie's face that amazed them most of all.

"Why, she's smiling so gently! And her cheeks are round and firm, like when she was my big sister, growing up in Haarlem!" exclaimed Corrie. "And oh, the peace and joy that is there!"

"She's gone home, Corrie," Mien said softly. "But oh, look at her face! She looks happy!"

And so it was! After a long moment, the women crept back to the barracks. Corrie went around the bunks telling the women who had known Betsie that she had been called home to heaven. She described in detail how beautiful Betsie had looked. The women cried because they had grown to love Betsie and they knew how much they would miss her. She had lived like Jesus. And she had shown them how He could bring light into even their darkest hours.

"But we're glad for Betsie, Corrie," a young woman explained. "She's safe at last from all this suffering. We're only crying for ourselves. We'll miss her so!"

"And we're crying for you, Corrie," said another. "We know how you must feel!"

How sad and lonely Corrie felt! She couldn't believe that Betsie had died.

"Even though there are hundreds of people all around me," she said to Mien, "I still feel so alone. I'm puzzled, too," she continued. "Betsie was so sure she would be released by Christmas and we would work together helping people who had been hurt by the war."

"Betsie *has* been released before Christmas," Mien pointed out. "She has been released from Ravensbruck and taken to God's house for higher service. Corrie, maybe you are the one who will fulfill Betsie's dream."

"It's nearly Christmas already," Corrie said doubtfully. "And it doesn't look as though anyone will escape."

But someone would.

11

Freedom

Hark checked his notes. It was now December 1944. The long roll call in the cold square was taking place. Twice each day all the women had to stand still while their names were called. The women shivered and tried to keep from freezing. Suddenly, Corrie jumped with shock.

"Cornelia ten Boom," boomed a voice through the loudspeakers. "Step to the side!" Terrified, Corrie obeyed.

"She is very scared," Hark wrote, hearing Corrie's anxious thoughts.

Maybe they've found out about the prayer meetings, Corrie worried. *Maybe I'm going to be punished! Who would have told them about our meetings?*

But then, after following a guard into the prison office, she was handed a slip of paper. On it a word was written: *Entlassungsschein.*[19]

Hark peered over Corrie's shoulder at the word. Angels speak every single language in the world. But even Hark had trouble with this extra-long word. Finally he made it out.

"She's being released," Hark whispered in awe.

Corrie was dazed, too. She could hardly believe it. Soon the gates of the prison camp were opened for her. As she left, she stuffed a day's ration of bread in her pocket. Then Corrie and some other released women were left at the station to wait for a train.

Hark was so, so happy! He jumped up and down with joy. Corrie was free! All the pain and suffering were finally over.

Almost.

Hark's spirits fell again as he watched Corrie feel in her coat pocket for her bread. Suddenly she sprang to her feet.

"It's gone!" she cried.

"Oh, no!" Hark exclaimed. He knew how awfully hungry Corrie was. The bread had either been lost or stolen. That meant she would have nothing to eat on the long train ride home.

Corrie rode for three days on a boxcar. When the train stopped, she tried to find someone who would give her food. But she had little luck. When the train finally arrived at Germany's border with Holland, Corrie was faint with hunger.

Hungry and wearing prison shoes that did not fit, she could hardly walk. Then she felt a strong arm around her. A kind man helped her cross the platform to another train. It took her safely over the border into Holland.

She was home. Even though Holland was still controlled by Germany, at least she was in her own country—her homeland.

Finally, she could rest—but not for long. There was work to be done and Betsie's dream to fulfill.

12

The Dream Comes True

After two weeks in the hospital, Corrie returned to her family. What laughter! What joy!

Sister Nollie's children had cleaned the Beje until it shone in honor of their Aunt Corrie's return. But once the party was over and Corrie settled down in Haarlem again, it just wasn't the same anymore. Corrie missed Betsie and Father. And even though the clock shop was still open, Corrie felt restless and unhappy.

One day she remembered what Betsie had said to her while they were still in the camp.

"A home, Corrie, for the broken ones . . . and our message about God's love in this darkness."[20]

That very week, Corrie began to tell that message to anyone who would listen.

"I can't keep up with this lady," chuckled Hark, flying along behind Corrie. His heavenly robe streamed out in the wind, and his clogs kept falling off at the fast pace!

On her trusty bicycle, Corrie bumped along the streets of Haarlem at a terrific rate. She was driven by the desire to tell everyone about God's enduring love.

In a few years churches all over the world would be asking her to come. People everywhere would want to hear how God had helped Corrie and Betsie in the prisons. Hark attended many of Corrie's early meetings. He liked to sit up front so he could see everyone. "I love to hear Corrie tell the story of Jesus and His love," he said happily to himself. "And I love to watch the faces of the people as they receive her wonderful message."

At the end of her talks Corrie would always share the first part of Betsie's dream. That was the part about a home in Holland where people who had been hurt by the war could learn to live again in peace.

Who's this? wondered Hark one day as a tall, slender lady came to talk to Corrie at the end of a meeting.

"I'm Mrs. Bierens de Haan," the lady said as if to answer Hark's question. "I'd like to help make Betsie's dream come true."

Corrie and Hark visited Mrs. Bierens de Haan's lovely earthly mansion. (*Pretty,* thought Hark, *but not nearly as beautiful as the mansions in heaven!*) Every detail of Betsie's dream was right there in front of their eyes. Hark's camera was working overtime. Betsie's dream was, indeed, coming true.

"Oh, what beautiful tulips," murmured Corrie.

"And here are the special wood floors and the statues," gasped Hark, busy with his camera.[21]

"It's just as I knew it would be," Corrie told Mrs. Bierens de Haan. The lovely lady looked surprised. "But how could you know what it would be like?" she asked. "Have you been here before?"

"No," Corrie said. Then she added silently, "but Betsie was here—in her dream." How else could she possibly explain that Betsie's dream had come true, to the last detail? She didn't think the woman would believe her.

At last Holland was freed from the Nazis. The Dutch people hung a flag from every window and celebrated their freedom. What a big party Holland had!

One day after the war Corrie was sharing her story with a group of people in Munich, Germany. A man came in and sat down near the front of the room. Hark recognized him at once. He was a guard from the prison camp!

What's he doing here? Hark wondered to himself in astonishment. Remembering how cruel this hateful man had been, Hark looked quickly to see if Corrie had noticed him.

What will she do if she sees him and remembers what he did to her and Betsie?

he wondered. Hark began to feel very hot and trembly, which always happened when he was nervous. Sometimes it even happened in the middle of choir practice when he saw a thousand hallelujahs coming up on his heavenly sheet music. He always wondered if he could sing them all without taking a heavenly breath. (And he always did!)

Turning his attention away from the heavenly choir, Hark went back to the job at hand. He heard Corrie say, "God filled my heart with love and forgiveness in Ravensbruck. You should forgive your enemies, too. God will help you," she promised.

She had not seen the guard. But at the end of meeting, the man walked up to Corrie and put his hand out to shake hers.

"Thank you for your message," he said. "It's wonderful isn't it, Sister Corrie, that Jesus has forgiven all our sins? Why, He's even forgiven *my* sins!"

Corrie went white. Now she recognized him! She couldn't take his hand. Suddenly she was thinking of all the things the cruel guards had done to them. Why, they had been partly responsible for Betsie's death! Hark could hear Corrie's thoughts quite clearly. He knew she was seeing all the horrible experiences she and Betsie had shared in the prison.

Hark waited breathlessly. "No one would blame her if she didn't shake the man's hand," he said out loud, as if his angel friends would agree with him. "After all, the man has done so many dreadful things, he doesn't deserve to be forgiven!"

But then, *no* human being deserved to be forgiven! And Jesus forgave them anyway!

Corrie was silently praying now. *Oh, Lord, help me to forgive him*, she said.

Her arm felt as heavy as lead. She couldn't raise it from her side to take the man's hand! But then a Scripture verse came to her mind. "God has poured out his love to fill our hearts."[22]

At last she prayed, *Oh, Jesus, I can't forgive him. But Your love within me can do it!*

Then, to her amazement, a warmth spread through her arm. She quickly clasped the former guard's hand, and her heart was filled with great love for him.

"Oh, Lord Jesus," she prayed, "thank You for giving me Your love when I don't have any of my own! All I need to do is ask You!"

God helped Corrie forgive those who had hurt her. He also helped her open the Beje as a home for the feeble-minded. And Mrs. Bierens de Haan's mansion was opened to war victims, too.

But the last part of Betsie's dream seemed to be quite impossible. Corrie wondered if Betsie had really been mistaken about converting a horrible camp into a home for war victims. Betsie had described this to Corrie when she was dying. It seemed so ridiculous. How could it possibly happen? How could a prison camp ever be filled with color and laughter? How could a place of death be turned into a place of healing and help?

Corrie didn't just work in Holland. After the war ended she also went to Germany to help the many homeless people. It was while she was sharing the love of Jesus there that Hark was able to finish his report.

A man who was organizing help for war victims came up to her and said, "We've found a place—in Germany. It's a former prison camp. Now that the war is over, the government wondered if you would help us. . . ."

He didn't finish. Corrie was smiling the widest smile he'd ever seen! And up in heaven, Corrie knew Betsie was smiling, too. God had made all her dreams come true!

The man drove Corrie (and Hark, though the man didn't know it) to a camp near Darmstadt.

Hark followed Corrie as she walked among the barracks. It was hard for her to see the narrow bunks lined up row after row. It made her remember all the pain she and Betsie had endured in a place like this. But thinking about Betsie reminded her of Betsie's dream.

"We must have flowers in all the windows—tulips, of course," Corrie said aloud.

"And then we'll paint it all the color of sunshine. It's time to paint the prisons bright!"

13

A Tulip in Heaven

Hark stayed up late that night, finishing his work. Then he traveled back through the stars to his home in heaven.

Before handing in his report, he made a list of facts that he thought C. D. already had. But he wanted to be sure, so he wrote them one by one:

1. Corrie traveled to sixty-four countries telling people about Jesus.

2. She wrote several books about her life. A movie was made about her story, too.

3. On her seventieth birthday, she

received a knighthood from Queen Juliana of The Netherlands.

4. In 1968, she was honored as "a righteous Gentile" by the government of Israel, the Jews' homeland.

5. She spent the last years of her life living quietly in California. A serious illness prevented her from traveling anymore.

"Corrie had her ninety-first birthday in heaven," Hark wrote with satisfaction as he finished his work. "On that very day, she entered the presence of the Lord she loved. What a wonderful birthday present!"

C. D. welcomed Hark back and thanked him for completing the work. He asked him if he had enjoyed the assignment. Hark paused, thinking of all the terrible things he had seen. But then he thought about Father ten Boom's family and especially Betsie and Corrie. They had loved their enemies as Jesus had loved His. They

forgave the people who had hurt them—as Jesus did. And they had won a victory over some of the Devil's worst and darkest work on earth. Remembering all this, Hark *was* glad, oh so glad, to have seen and recorded it all!

After he had handed his report to C. D., Hark went home and hung up his little clogs. He painted the Dutch tulip he had brought back with him with some heavenly paint that would keep it fresh forever. Then he planted the tulip in his garden. It would always remind him of his adventures and all he had learned of the power and help his Master had given to His two very special servants!

Then Hark hurried off to choir practice—to sing a few thousand hallelujahs to his King!

Corrie ten Boom

References and Notes

References

Some of the information for this story was provided by Pamela Rosewell Moore, Corrie ten Boom's former companion and now curator of the Corrie ten Boom Collection at Dallas Baptist University in Dallas, Texas. Other details were supplied by Geni Preisser, a hostess for the Beje in Haarlem, The Netherlands. In addition, the following books about Corrie ten Boom were used as references.

Notes

1. Corrie ten Boom with Carole C. Carlson, *In My Father's House* (Old Tappan, N.J.: Fleming H. Revell, 1976), p. 117.

2. Corrie ten Boom, *A Prisoner and Yet* (Fort Washington, Pa.: Christian Literature Crusade, 1954), p. 14.

3. Survivor's account, cited in Carole C. Carlson, *Corrie ten Boom: Her Life, Her Faith* (Old Tappan, N.J.: Fleming H. Revell, 1983), p. 93.

4. Corrie ten Boom, *A Prisoner and Yet,* p. 22.

5. See Corrie ten Boom with Jamie Buckingham, *Tramp for the Lord* (New York: Jove Books, 1978), p. 94.

6. Corrie ten Boom with John and Elizabeth Sherrill, *The Hiding Place* (Washington Depot, Conn: Chosen Books, Fleming H. Revell Co., 1971), p. 143.

7. This event is described, with variations, in *A Prisoner and Yet; The Hiding Place; Corrie ten Boom: Her Life and Faith;* and other books by or about Corrie ten Boom.

8. The story of Betsie's prayers bringing peace to the crowded

barracks is told in *A Prisoner and Yet,* p. 115–16; *He Sets the Captives Free,* p. 23–24; and *The Hiding Place,* p. 182.

9. Joan Winmill Brown, *Corrie: The Lives She's Touched* (Old Tappan, N. J.: Fleming H. Revell, 1979), p. 61.

10. 1 Thessalonians 5:14–15 and 16–18. The reading of these verses is described in *The Hiding Place,* p. 180.

11. The sisters' decision to be thankful for the fleas and lice in the barracks is described in Kjersti Hoff Baez's book, *Corrie ten Boom* (Westwood, N.J.: Barbour and Co., 1989), p. 180, and in *The Hiding Place,* 180–81, 190.

12. Corrie ten Boom, *He Sets the Captives Free* (Old Tappan, N.J.: Fleming H. Revell, 1977), p. 18.

13. Romans 8:35–37. The reading of these verses is described in *The Hiding Place,* p. 177–78.

14. Matthew 28:20. The reading of these verses is described in *He Sets the Captives Free,* p. 19.

15. Corrie ten Boom, *In My Father's House*, p. 192.

16. 1 Kings 17:10–16. This story is mentioned in *The Hiding Place,* p. 184.

17. Corrie tells the story of the oil in *A Prisoner and Yet,* p. 108–9, and in *The Hiding Place,* p. 184–85.

18. The sisters' dreams and plans for their lives after Ravensbruck are described in several books by or about Corrie, including *The Hiding Place; Corrie ten Boom: Her Life, Her Faith; Tramp for the Lord;* and *He Sets the Captives Free.*

19. Corrie ten Boom, *A Prisoner and Yet,* p. 88.

20. Carole C. Carlson, *Corrie ten Boom: Her Life, Her Faith,* p. 120.

21. The house is described in *Corrie ten Boom: Her Life, Her Faith*, p. 125; in *The Hiding Place,* p. 212–13; and in *A Prisoner and Yet,* p. 175.

22. Romans 5:5. In her book, *Tramp for the Lord,* p. 78, Corrie recalls using this verse to help her forgive her former guard. This event also is described in *The Hiding Place,* and in Corrie's book, *Clippings from My Notebook* (Thorndike, Me.: Thorndike Press, 1982).

For Further Reading

We recommend these additional books about the life of Corrie ten Boom. Look for them at your library or bookstore.

Kjersti Hoff Baez. *Corrie ten Boom*. Westwood, N.J.: Barbour and Co., 1989. (A children's book.)

Joan Winmill Brown. *Corrie: The Lives She's Touched*. Old Tappan, N.J.: Fleming H. Revell, 1979.

Carole C. Carlson. *Corrie ten Boom: Her Life, Her Faith*. Old Tappan, N.J.: Fleming H. Revell, 1983.

Corrie ten Boom. *A Prisoner and Yet*. Fort Washington, Pa.: Christian Literature Crusade, 1954.

Corrie ten Boom with John and Elizabeth Sherrill. *The Hiding Place*. Washington Depot, Conn: Chosen Books, Fleming H. Revell, 1971.

Corrie ten Boom with Carole C. Carlson. *In My Father's House*. Old Tappan, N.J.: Fleming H. Revell, 1976.

Corrie ten Boom. *He Sets the Captives Free*. Old Tappan, N.J.: Fleming H. Revell, 1977.

Corrie ten Boom with Jamie Buckingham. *Tramp for the Lord*. New York: Jove Books, 1978.

Corrie ten Boom. *Father ten Boom, God's Man*. Old Tappan, N.J.: Fleming H. Revell, 1979.

Corrie ten Boom. *Clippings from My Notebook*. Thorndike, Me.: Thorndike Press, 1982.

Pamela Rosewell. *The Five Silent Years of Corrie ten Boom*. Grand Rapids, Mich., Zondervan, 1986.